LADYBIRD
LONDON
SEARCH AND FIND

Illustrated by Klara Hawkins

LADYBIRD BOOKS is part of the
Penguin Random House group of companies
whose addresses can be found at global.penguinrandomhouse.com.

Penguin
Random House
UK

First published 2019
001
Illustrated by Klara Hawkins
Copyright © Ladybird Books Ltd, 2019
Printed in China
ISBN: 978–0–241–37077–3
All correspondence to:
Ladybird Books, Penguin Random House Children's
80 Strand, London WC2R 0RL

CONTENTS

THE HOUSES OF PARLIAMENT

Officially called the Palace of Westminster, politicians meet in the Houses of Parliament to make important decisions. In the cloakroom, purple ribbons are attached to the coat-hangers because members of parliament used to hang their swords from them.

POLICE

POLICE

THAMES CRUISE

TOWER BRIDGE   42

CAN YOU FIND . . .?

1 clock
2 police officers
3 red buses
5 Union Jack flags

BIG BEN

Many people think the clock tower is called Big Ben, but that's actually the name of the bell inside the tower. The huge iron bell arrived in a carriage drawn by sixteen white horses, after being carried down the River Thames in a big boat.

THE BIG SHIPPING CO.

Westminster Whizzers

REGENT'S PARK   205

COVENT GARDEN   77

COVENT GARDEN

LIVING STATUE

The name 'Covent Garden' came about because of a spelling mistake! It was supposed to be 'Convent Garden', the market garden of the convent of Westminster Abbey.

CAN YOU FIND . . . ?

1 painter
2 red telephone boxes
5 juggling balls
6 vases of flowers

There are many amazing street performers in Covent Garden. They juggle, sing, do magic and perform tricks. Some even dress up as gold or silver statues and stay still for hours without moving, eating, drinking or going to the toilet!

BUCKINGHAM PALACE

Buckingham Palace is the official London home of Queen Elizabeth II. The palace has 775 rooms, including hundreds of bedrooms and 78 bathrooms. It even has its own post office and police station.

CAN YOU FIND . . .?

1 hot-air balloon
3 ice-cream cones
5 dogs
10 guards

On your visit you might see the Changing of the Guard – a grand ceremony where the Queen's Guard swap places. You'll easily spot them in their tall bearskin hats and bright red jackets, marching up and down.

LONDON ZOO

In one corner of Regent's Park is London Zoo.
There are lots of amazing animals here. You might
even spot the cheeky pelicans who usually live in
Regent's Park but have a habit of flying into
the zoo for extra food!

ice cream

LONDON ZOO

THE RIVER THAMES

The River Thames runs through the centre of London. On the northern side you can see a curved glass tower known as the Gherkin. It got this nickname because it looks a bit like a pickle!

Beside the Gherkin is the Tower of London, which used to be a prison. If you visit, you can see the Crown Jewels, meet the castle's ravens and hear tales of kings, queens and treason.

THE GHERKIN

THE TOWER OF LONDON

THAMES CRUISE

LADYBIRD

In central London, the Thames is tidal. This means the water rises and falls every day like it does in the sea.

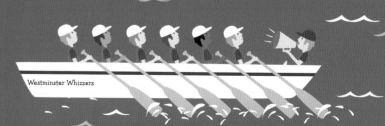

Westminster Whizzers

CAN YOU FIND . . .?

1 crown
2 red cranes
3 ravens
4 boats

THE SHARD

The Shard is currently the tallest building in Britain. You can ride a lift right up to the top and look out over London.

TOWER BRIDGE

Tower Bridge is one of London's most famous bridges. It can lift up to allow tall boats to sail under it.

HMS BELFAST

The HMS Belfast is an old ship Britain used during wars. It's now a museum, so it's safe for you to go in.

13

TRAFALGAR SQUARE

Trafalgar Square was named after the Battle of Trafalgar, which took place in 1805. There are statues in the square, on tall pillars called plinths. One of the plinths, known as the 'Fourth Plinth', is used to display modern statues and pieces of art.

NELSON'S COLUMN

CHARLES JAMES NAPIER
GENERAL

Nelson's Column is at the centre of Trafalgar Square.
Nelson was a senior commander called an admiral,
who fought bravely and died in the Battle of Trafalgar.
The column is guarded by four enormous bronze lions.

The National Gallery sits along one side of Trafalgar
Square and contains over two thousand famous paintings,
including works by Vincent van Gogh and Michelangelo.

CAN YOU FIND . . . ?

1 person in a fountain
2 crying babies
7 people taking photographs
15 pigeons

NATIONAL GALLERY

MAJOR GENERAL
SIR HENRY HAVELOCK

GUIDE

GUIDE

THE SOUTH BANK AND THE LONDON EYE

This is the South Bank. As you might have guessed, it stretches along the south bank of the River Thames! It is a place of art and culture, and is full of restaurants, theatres and market stalls.

HOT DOGS

ice cream

FAIRGROUND

CAN YOU FIND . . . ?

1 umbrella

2 pairs of binoculars

4 people holding hot dogs

4 people on skateboards

COFFEE

The London Eye is like an enormous fairground wheel. From the top, on a clear day, you can see all across London. Nearly four million people go on the London Eye each year.

BOROUGH MARKET

FRESH JUICE

APPLE APPLE APPLE APPLE APPLE APPLE

BUNS A

FRUIT FRUIT FRUIT

FRESH LEMONS

Borough Market is one of the oldest food markets in London. It opens at ten o'clock on weekdays and eight o'clock on Saturdays – but some traders, bakers and delivery drivers are here from two o'clock in the morning!

TOMATOES   RED CABBAGES

THE LONDON UNDERGROUND

You can travel around London on the London Underground.
The Underground is often known as 'the Tube', because the
long, narrow trains zoom through tunnels underneath the city.

There are eleven different Tube lines . . . each one has a different name and is shown in a different colour on the Underground map.

WAY OUT

Visit the London Eye

THE ALLERY

young artists
exhibition

LONDO

TRAVE

Underground trains travel 43 million miles every year. That's almost halfway to the sun!

There are old Underground stations all over London that are no longer used – they're known as 'ghost stations'.

CAN YOU FIND . . . ?
1 WAY OUT sign
2 red balloons
4 people wearing headphones
4 suitcases

THE ROYAL OBSERVATORY

Learn about the stars and time at the Royal Observatory in Greenwich.
Many, many years ago, scientists at the Royal Observatory looked
through telescopes and drew maps of the stars in the sky.

CAN YOU FIND . . . ?

1 bicycle
2 kites
4 people wearing watches
7 ice-cream cones

There is a brass line on the ground outside the Royal Observatory, which shows something called 'the prime meridian' – an imaginary line that astronomers drew across the world to work out what time it should be in different parts of the world. The clock time at the Royal Observatory is called Greenwich Mean Time (GMT).

ST PAUL'S CATHEDRAL

St Paul's Cathedral is one of the most impressive buildings in London. It was built by Sir Christopher Wren, one of Britain's most famous architects, and took more than 30 years to build. The cathedral was declared officially complete on Christmas Day in 1711.

In the cathedral there's an area called the **Whispering Gallery**, where even your quietest whisper can be heard on the other side of the gallery. *Sssh!*

LIVERPOOL STREET

TAXI

TAXI

SHAKESPEARE'S GLOBE THEATRE

CAN YOU FIND . . . ?

1 skull
2 people crying
9 people wearing glasses
10 hats

Many people consider William Shakespeare (1564-1616) to be the greatest playwright of all time. Shakespeare's Globe is a circular open-air theatre, built as an exact copy of the original theatre in which his plays were first performed. You can stand to watch a performance or you can sit in the seats around the edge.

There is no roof above where the audience stands, so beware: if it rains during the show people can get very wet!

CHINATOWN

GERRARD STREET W1
爵祿街

CHINA GIFTS

NOODLES

SHANGHAI SPICE

OPEN

MENU
Fish 2
Fish 3
Special
Fancy Fish 4
Special

MENU
Dim Sum 6
Egg 3
Noodles
Fried 4
Rice

CAN YOU FIND . . . ?

1 dragon
2 street signs
4 restaurants
7 sets of people
holding hands

Chinatown is an area of London near Leicester Square where there are a lot of Chinese restaurants and businesses. It is a very colourful area – you will see many beautiful lanterns hanging above you as you walk around. There are lots of festivals and events during the year where you can watch traditional parades and eat delicious Chinese food.

CHINATOWN

GERRARD STREET W1
爵祿街

RED DRAGON RESTAURANT

Menu
Spiced Rice   5
Chilli Chicken 6
Spring Rolls   7

THE NATURAL HISTORY MUSEUM

DINOSAURS

TOILETS

The Natural History Museum is filled with incredible sights, such as the enormous skeleton of a blue whale, the largest creature that's ever lived. Her name is Hope.

Other fascinating things to spot at the museum include the first T-rex fossil ever discovered, a crystallized nugget of gold, and a meteorite from Mars. There's even an earthquake simulator so you can feel the power and strength of a real earthquake!

Blue Whale

CAN YOU FIND . . .?
1 child dressed as a dinosaur
3 babies in buggies
4 pictures of a blue whale
10 people taking photographs

MAMMALS →

At the Natural History Museum you can learn about how life on our planet has evolved – from the very earliest forms of life on Earth right up to the world we live in today.

Blue Whale

ANSWERS

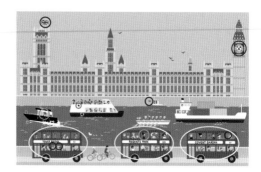

4–5 THE HOUSES OF PARLIAMENT AND BIG BEN

6–7 COVENT GARDEN

8–9 BUCKINGHAM PALACE

10–11 LONDON ZOO

12–13 THE RIVER THAMES

14–15 TRAFALGAR SQUARE

16–17 THE SOUTH BANK AND THE LONDON EYE

18–19 BOROUGH MARKET

20–21 THE LONDON UNDERGROUND

22–23 THE ROYAL OBSERVATORY

24–25 ST PAUL'S CATHEDRAL

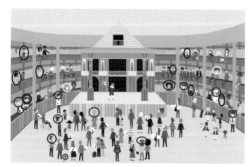

26–27 SHAKESPEARE'S GLOBE THEATRE

28–29 CHINATOWN

30–31 THE NATURAL HISTORY MUSEUM